I0473241

Angelic Rx's for Manifesting

An Adult Coloring Book

"I am thrilled to introduce you to our new series of Angelic Rx Adult Coloring Books for Relaxation. Our first in the series, "Angelic Rx's for Manifesting," allows you to experience the wisdom of the angels while you focus on manifesting your hearts desires.

Inside you'll find 20 amazing art activities that will take you to a calm, peaceful and happy place of relaxed coloring bliss. These angelic images offer an easy way to de-stress and unleash your inner artist. Plus, each one has a message from the angels to assist you in your manifestation journey."

-- Epigenetic Healing Artist,

Lori Daniel Falk

Author & Artist, Lori Daniel Falk

This edition first published in the USA by Wisdom of the Angels

Madison, WI

All rights reserved.

No part of this book may be reproduced or utilized

in any form or by any means, electronic or mechanical,

without prior permission in writing from the Publishers.

Copyright © 2016 Lori Daniel Falk

All rights reserved.

ISBN:9780692683125
ISBN- 10: 0692683127

www.wisdomoftheangels.com

DEDICATION

This book is dedicated to Earth Angels everywhere who help the world just by being their magnificent selves. Who are Earth Angels you might ask? Earth Angels are anyone who lives their life from a place of love. Who encompasses a deep abiding desire to make the world a better place. Who are willing to dive deep within their own psyche and the psyche of others to find the truth. Many have an innate understanding of the potential and magic of the Universe, and simply cannot rest until all the world knows about it.

In honor of my father, Albert P. Liske, Artist Extraordinaire …

"Those who work with their hands are laborers.

Those who work with their hands and heads are craftsmen.

Those who work with their hands, their heads, and their hearts are artists."

Thank you for sharing your wisdom, your heart and your gifts with me daddy. I love you.

CONTENTS

ACKNOWLEDGMENTS

As this book goes to press and I think of who I want to thank, the answer is simple. It is all of you. All of my many wonderful clients who over the years have shared their wishes and hearts desires with me. For as you have done this, you have given me the inspiration to create products, and programs and art designed to help you achieve those very wishes and desires. My only goal has been to create the ways and means for your hearts to open, and then to heal.
As it is through the heart that you can heal your mind, your body and your soul.

I also want to thank my amazing assistant Debbie Klineschmidt for her endless dedication and commitment to the mission of bringing peace to the world one heart at a time. Without her none of this would have been possible. She is quite simply "the wind beneath my wings." My heart is filled with gratitude as I know how truly blessed I am to have her on this journey with me.

And then there's my other Earth Angel, my puppy, Tallie Ann. This art came into the world when she came into my life. In fact, you will note that all of my art pieces have hearts within them. Tallie actually has a heart on her right side. It's as if the angels wanted the world to know that she is nothing but one hundred percent pure love. Her tireless dedication to assist in this work has never gone unnoticed or unappreciated. She is my heart. She is my love.
And again, I am so truly, truly blessed.

INTRODUCTION

The Joy of Coloring

Why do we so love to color? Think of it this way, "Coloring in a book doesn't require artistic training to get started, yet it offers a great sense of accomplishment when finishing a piece." Many people liken coloring to yoga or meditation. It's the perfect antidote to all the multitasking most of us do all day long. When it's time to relax at the end of the day many of us feel guilty for sitting down and just watching TV. So we text, we knit, we paint our nails, we scroll through Facebook, and now apparently we color too. God forbid we'd say it's OK to be "lazy" when we're trying to relax !?!?!? Most importantly of all, it gets us out of the digital world and into reality … OMG you gotta admit we need more of that.

It also appears there's a big social aspect to this coloring trend that many new fans find appealing. A recent search of the social media world found that when you put the #coloring hashtag into Instagram 1,079,251 posts come up. There are numerous Adult Coloring Facebook groups as well, some with as many as 40,000 plus members. Seems people all over the world are sharing their finished pieces of art on social media sites like Instagram, Pinterest and Twitter … and many are doing it (Coloring, that is) in social settings like Coloring Clubs, that meet at both homes and coffee shops alike. (I gotta tell you … working as much as I do, I would much prefer a Coloring Club to a Book Club any day … and that is NOT just because I'm in artist, it's because I need to relax!?!) Face it, coloring is a fun way to get together and do something that engages a little bit of your creative side, but allows you to talk, hang out, drink coffee … or maybe even have a glass of wine, or two!

The Joy of Coloring with the Angels

"What we're about to begin here today is not magic, but it is quite magical. And it is quite significant … it is intended to dramatically improve the quality of your life as you will have the 'Wisdom of the Angels' at your fingertips at all times." Lest you think what we're about to do here is a bit out of the ordinary, consider the following statistics …

- The majority of the people in the world believe in angels. Somewhere between 77 to 88% of Americans alone believe in Angels.

- Angels are found in just about every religion and culture.

- One recent survey found that more than 32% of Americans said they have encountered an angel and nearly 2/3rds of widows have had an experience with their deceased husbands.

- More than half of all adults believe that they have been protected by a guardian angel at some point during their life.

.

The Joy of Angelic Rx's

Want to hear something exciting?

According to the latest science, we can have a huge positive impact on our health simply by improving our thoughts, emotions and beliefs. How cool is that!?!

Seems it's not just the DNA alone that creates disease, rather it's the beliefs we hold as true. Craziest part is that those pesky beliefs are often not even our own, rather they are the beliefs we were taught by our parents and grandparents and even our great grandparents that create our "multi-generational Emotional DNA" if you will.

Say what?!? Seriously, they are now discovering that children who are adopted often end up contracting the same ailments as their adopted parents. Yup, no blood line created DNA there ... just beliefs, habits and "learned" ways of being. And as I always say, "The good thing about learned behavior, is that it can be unlearned and relearned ... in a much healthier way!?!"

This *Angelic Rx's for Manifesting Adult Coloring Book* allows you to experience the wisdom of the angels while you focus on manifesting your hearts desires. Inside you'll find 20 amazing art activities that will take you to a calm, peaceful and happy place of coloring bliss. These angelic images offer an easy way to de-stress and unleash your inner artist. Plus, each one has a message from the angels to assist you in the manifestation, or attraction of, your deepest hopes and dreams.

The images are all in GRAY-SCALE, optimized for coloring. You can use the gray tones as a guide to add depth and dimension to your unique coloring style.

The Joy of Coloring with Lori … and the Angels

The angels, those unconditionally loving, benevolent beings of light that surround all of us, want nothing more than to hold our hearts and gently guide us through these interesting, and sometimes challenging times we are living in. As messengers of God, they carry the divine wisdom of the ages. Seeking their guidance not only makes sense, it seems the only sensible thing to do. So that's what I did. I centered myself in a meditative state and attuned with the angels and then simply asked them, "What do the people of the world need to know about things like manifesting their hearts desires and the life of their dreams." (How I even became a visionary artist is a whole other story, and quite an interesting one I might add. To learn more about it visit www.wisdomoftheangels.com)

One of the first things they told me was, "*they want to make life easier for all of us.*" It is with that in mind, that they encode the Angelic Message Portraits I co-create with them, with the energy of their infinite wisdom. The portraits I create are designed to work with you at a heart level, enabling you to assimilate their knowledge directly into your emotional field, bypassing your cognitive mind, and enabling you instant access to it, without the need for total intellectual comprehension. That's a mouthful (they tend to be a bit intellectual in their explanations … lol). What it means in layman's terms is you literally get infused with divine wisdom when you're playing with this art.

That's the best part … While you are relaxing and fully enjoying yourself and having fun coloring the angels in this book, some key things are happening. You are working with art that is encoded with angelic healing energy. You are bringing it to life with your colors, and you are raising your emotional state and in turn your vibrational frequency to the level necessary to create more love, joy, health, wealth, peace and happiness in your life. In so doing you will begin to effortlessly draw your dreams right into your new more relaxed life, creating a whole new reality for yourself.

Manifesting With the Angels

We are constantly manifesting or attracting things into our lives. Every thought we have is a prayer. Every emotion we experience is an even stronger prayer. As these thoughts and emotions go out into the world they attract back to us what we are feeling and focusing on. It's really that simple. Many call this, "The Law of Attraction." Bottom line is that it's always happening. So you can either let that happen unconsciously by not caring or thinking about it. Or you can decide to consciously choose your thoughts to create the life you've always been dreaming of. The angels and I will show you how through the messages and art you are about to experience.

May this book be only the beginning of all your dreams coming true. Let it be the tipping point that leads you to grander, and greater and even more amazing life adventures.

From my heart to yours ~ Lori

Manifesting Your Dreams ... It's Easy

~ All it Takes is 17 Seconds ~

Some of you may have heard of the Law of Attraction, others may not have. Since it's a principle of manifesting, I thought it prudent to mention it in this book. Put simply, the Law of Attraction states that what we focus on is what we attract more of. If we focus on good, we attract more good. If we focus on negativity, we attract more negativity. What we send out, is what we attract more of. It's really this simple ... like attracts like.

So follow these 7 simple rules and watch your dreams come true.

Rule #1 ~ STAY FOCUSED ... Always focus on what you want, not what you don't want.

Rule #2 ~ IDENTIFY ... Decide what it is you are truly desiring to attract into your life.

Rule #3 ~ IMAGINATION ... Imagine what it feels like to have this in your life now.

Rule #4 ~ FEEL ... Determine how you will feel when you actually have attracted your dream.

Rule #5 ~ EXPECT ... Do not waver. Expect your dream to come true. You do NOT need to know how, you only need to get out of the way and allow the universe to creatively bring this to you.

Rule #6 ~ GRATITUDE ... Practice an attitude of gratitude for all the good that already exists in your life ... especially in related areas of your life.

Rule #7 ~ 17 SECONDS ... Once a day spend 17 seconds imagining the feeling of having what it is you are wanting already in your life. Get super stoked and excited about it as if it's already there. Feel the feelings of joy and exhilaration you will experience when it has arrived. The key here is this must be 17 seconds of pure undiluted focus with no room for doubt, questioning or concern about HOW it will appear. Be like a child and simply DAYDREAM for 17 seconds.

It truly is that simple. Now go play, daydream AND COLOR, COLOR, COLOR. The relaxed state of mind achieved through coloring is just what you need to help make Your Dreams Come True!

ENJOY!

A Prayer to the Angels

As you begin to color I encourage you to center yourself and recite the following prayer ...

Close your eyes and take several deep breaths into your heart ...
And know that this is your time, time to let go of all the cares in the world
And just let the angels envelope you in their wings.

As you're breathing into your heart, let's call in Archangel Michael ...
Michael we ask you to join us now, and surround us in a bubble of white light,
Divine Christ like energy,
Allowing in only messages and beings that are 100% pure love and light.

Next we call in the Golden Light Angels
And we ask you Golden Light Angels to surround this white light
With an extra layer of liquid gold light energy,
The strongest protection in the Universe.

And from this safe and sacred space, we call in Archangel Raphael ...
Raphael we ask you to fill our hearts with all the unconditional love of the angelic realm.
So that this love might surround us and infuse us,
and touch the hearts of all whom we encounter.

Now let's call in Archangel Gabrielle ...
Gabrielle we ask that you help us to hear crystal clear divine communication.
That you inspire us with exactly what we need to know
to experience a life filled with more love, joy, health, wealth, peace and happiness.

Finally we call in Archangel Uriel ...
Uriel we ask that you help us keep our thoughts and emotions
vibrating at a high, high frequency
so that we might attract wonderful, glorious, amazing things into our lives.

And lastly, we take a moment to express our deepest, deepest gratitude
for all of this divine angelic assistance that is with us now,
as it is every day of our lives. All we ever need do is ASK.

And so it is. Thanks be to God.

Remember ... the angels can only help if you ASK!

THE MANIFESTATION ANGEL

Here's a Message from the Manifestation Angel ...

- What is it that wants to spring forth from the depths of your soul?

- What wants to be born?

- What's trying to emerge?

- What is your heart simply yearning for?

These inspirations and seeds of ideas were planted in your heart for a reason. They've been inspired by your spirit, that greater part of yourself that remembers your very reason for being, and they're ready to burst into bloom. They're simply waiting for you to say, "YES!"

This Manifestation Angel reminds us that as co-creative forces in this grand playground called Earth, we have the innate ability to live the life of our dreams. All we truly need do is set the intention to create anew, focus on how amazing we will feel when this new creation takes form in our lives, and allow the universe to do the rest.

So RELAX and DAYDREAM as you color her beautiful ...

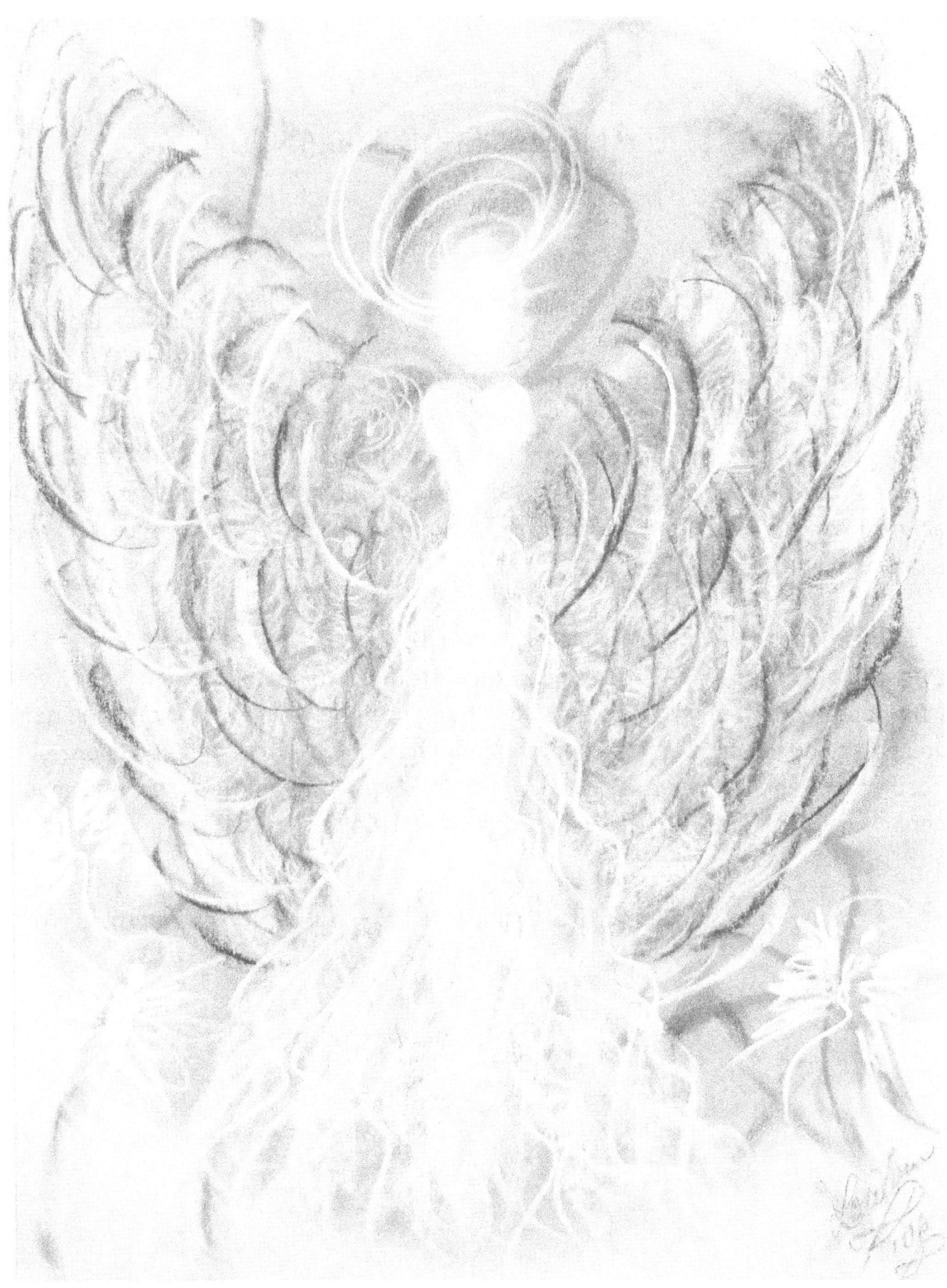

THE ANGEL OF ABUNDANCE

A Message from the Angel of Abundance ...

The Angel of Abundance reminds us that the Law of Attraction is in action at all times. Similar to the Law of Gravity, it just is. With that in mind it is important to note that you can only attract things into your life that are in alignment with your current emotional state or vibrational frequency. So not only is it important for us to watch our thoughts, we must monitor our emotions as well.

She explains it like this, "If every thought is a prayer, every emotion is an even stronger prayer." To attract unlimited abundance into your life you must keep your thoughts and emotions high. Let the Angel of Abundance help you raise yours now. Let her help you "eliminate negativity" and focus on your desires instead of fears, "practice the fine art of forgiveness," and most important of all, let her help you adopt an attitude of gratitude.

*A*s you color this angel beautiful think of all the things you are grateful for!

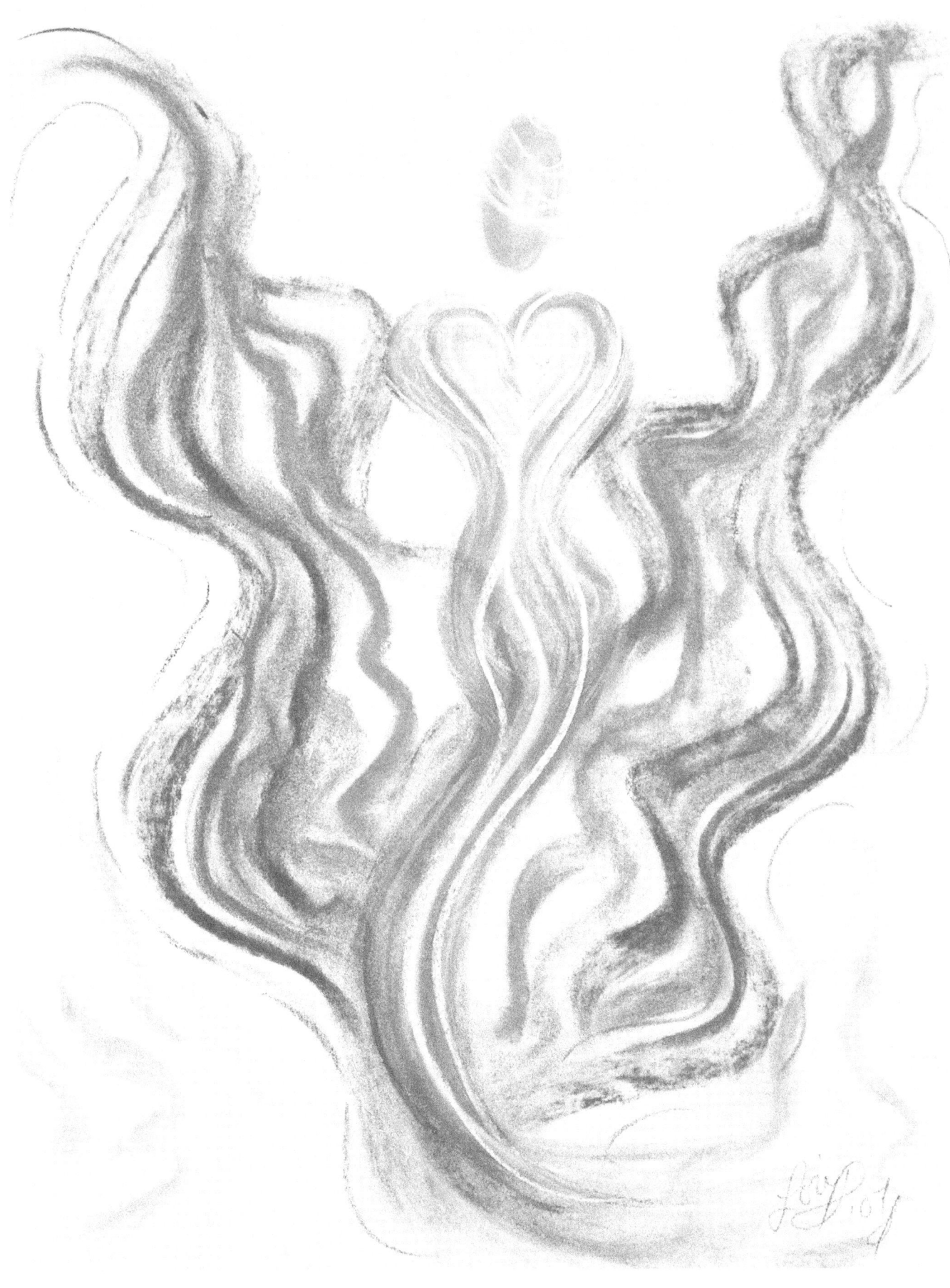

THE SEDONA MAGIC ANGEL

A Message from the Red Rock Vortex's of Sedona ...

This Angel was created in Sedona, Arizona, a place long known for both it's spirituality and it's beauty.

This angel is infused with the magic of Sedona's spiritual vortex energies along with the emotional healing power and strength of the Angels. You could say it's been injected with just what is needed to move YOU at a heart level to bring forth that which you so truly desire.

This piece of art serves as a powerful manifestation tool, a visual meditation vehicle and spiritual connector.

So go ahead and infuse her with the colors that light up your life.

THE ENLIGTENMENT ANGEL

A Message for you from the Enlightenment Angel ...

To even begin to reach enlightenment one must not just realize, but accept the fact that everything is, and always will be in divine order. With that in mind it is of paramount importance that we look at what seems to be bad, or wrong, or hurtful . . . all those feelings of unpleasantness . . . and find the gift that lies within.

One could almost say it's as simple as knowing that when something seemingly "bad" shows up, it's merely showing us what it is we are really wanting. Think of the old saying, "To err is human, but to forgive is divine." You'll know you are truly in touch with your "God-self" when you have the ability to look adversity in the face and lovingly embrace it.

So imagine that "It's all good," as you color your cares away ...

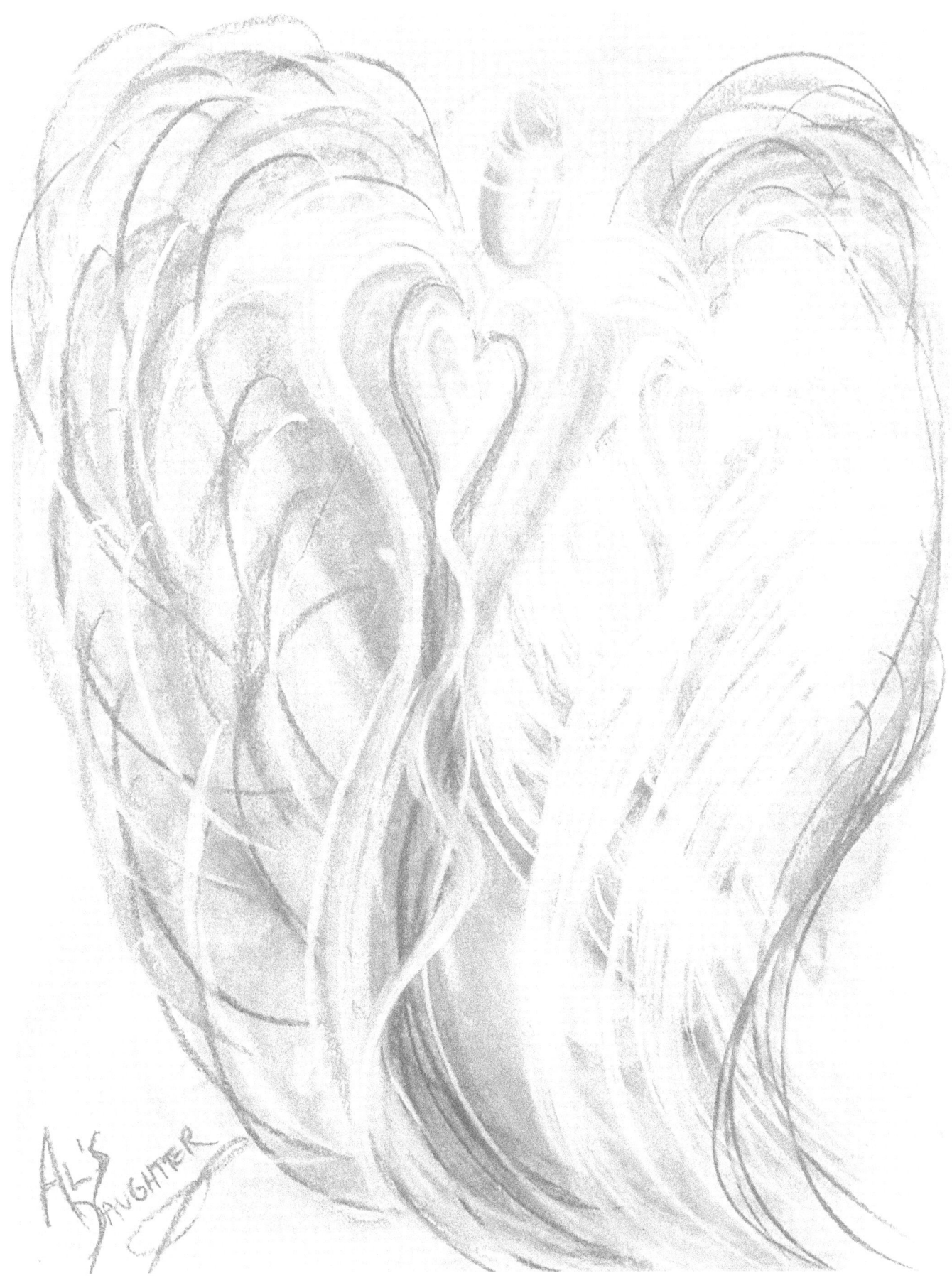

THE CHAKRA ANGEL

The Chakra Angel's Message for You...

Are your charkas balanced? Say what? Your chakras are these little energy centers throughout your body that send out messages to the world about who you really are and how you're feeling. More importantly they'll let the world know if you're relaxed or stressed like crazy. To fully manifest what you most desire into your life you need to be relaxed and balanced.

The only thing stopping us is our old wounding. It's up to us to heal those wounds and open our hearts to allow this in. We must call on the angels, to assist us in removing the old obstacles ... to assist us in our own spiritual, evolutionary journeys.

So pick your favorite colors and show the world who you really are ...

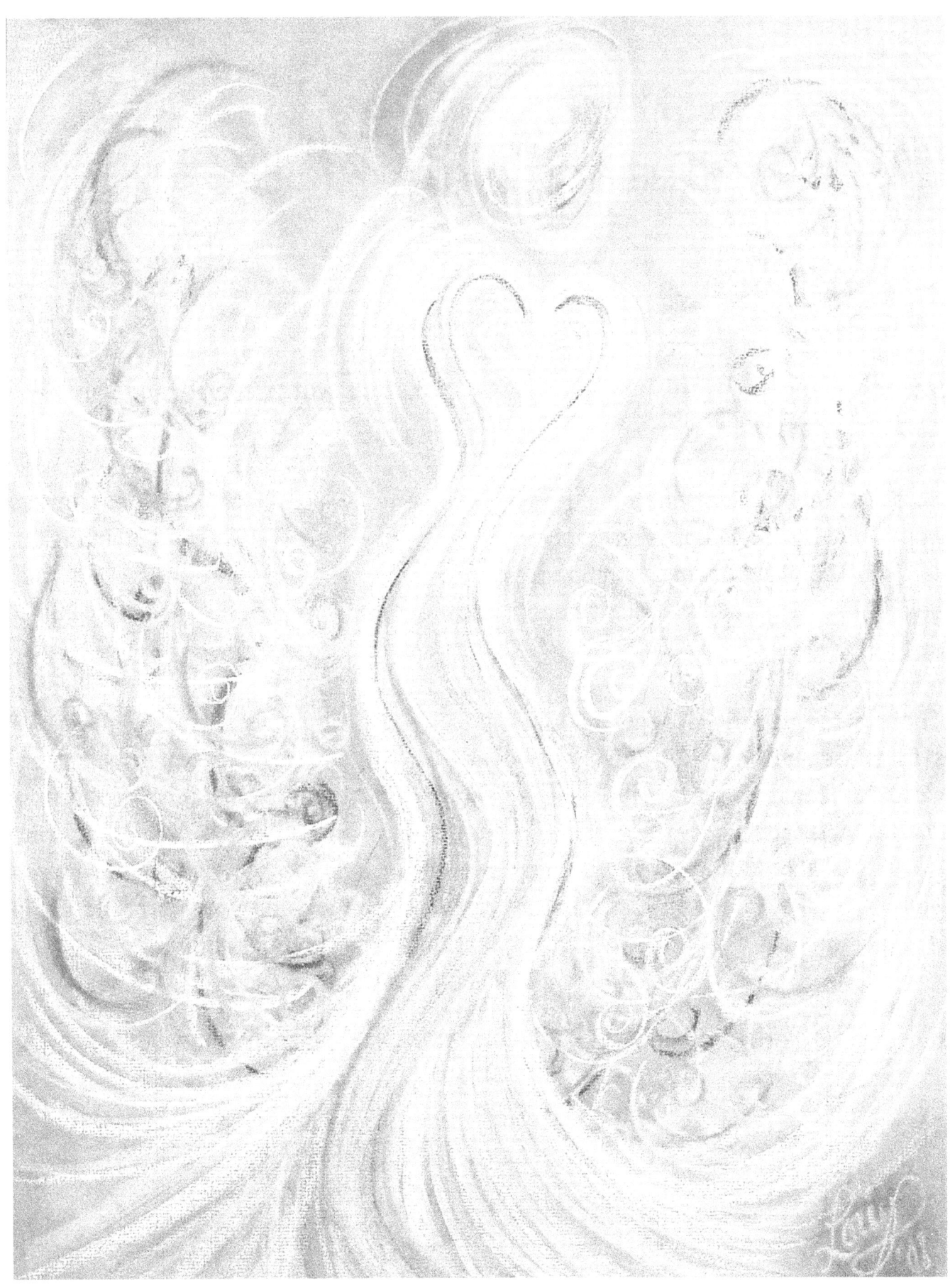

THE ACTIVATION ANGEL

The Activation Angel's Message ...

My experience with this angel is simply that it activates everything it is near ... specifically YOU!

So color her brilliant and hang her in your home, your office, anywhere in you want to amp things up. Want more social activity, hang her in your living room or great room. Looking to amp up your love life, try hanging her above your bed. Dreaming of more clients or increased sales, then the office just might be the place.

Then watch as things begin to take on a life of their own. Nothing seems to stay the same once it's been "activated" by this angel. Your world will seem more expansive, your life purpose more intensely significant, your life somehow is just not the same. There's an intensity energetically pouring from this angel that simply will not allow things to be status quo. So if you want to shake things up a bit ... or if you want to make a bigger difference in this world ... then the Activation Angel is quite simply your gal!

Let the activation begin with brilliantly intense, gloriously vibrant colors ...

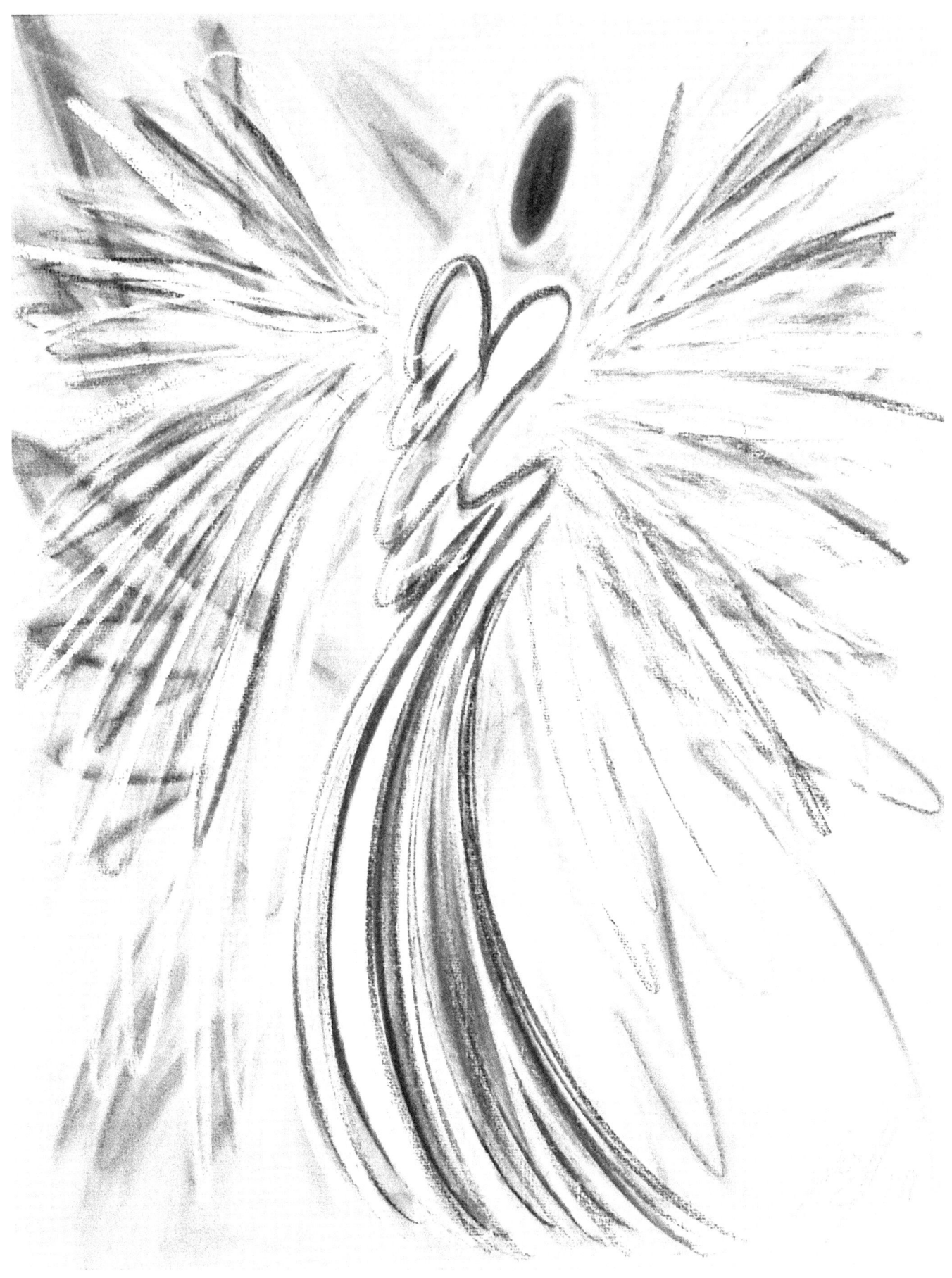

EVOLVING INTO WHOLENESS ANGEL

It happened very spontaneously on a Sunday afternoon …

Without even thinking about it I had put on some beautiful, yet intense, Classical music. Seems the art was crescendoing right along with the notes of the music. Plus, in addition to the "usual folks" who assist me with this work, from the Ascended Masters to the Golden Light Angels, this time Master Healer, Jesus was clearly present as well.

As the session was progressing, my client shared with me that, with her eyes closed, she could feel which part of the Angel Portrait I was working on. In fact she said, "It felt like a new energy configuration was being painted directly into her physical being as she could literally feel each brush stroke." When it was complete, she said that of all the energy/spiritual work she's done over the years, nothing had been quite as intense as this.

I've named this piece "Evolving Into Wholeness" as it seemed only appropriate based on the Angelic Message that came through. As my client is also a dear friend, I have had the privilege of witnessing some amazing transformations that are coming into fruition for her in the time since we shared this process together. I am beyond proud of her!

Color away and let this Angel do the same for you.

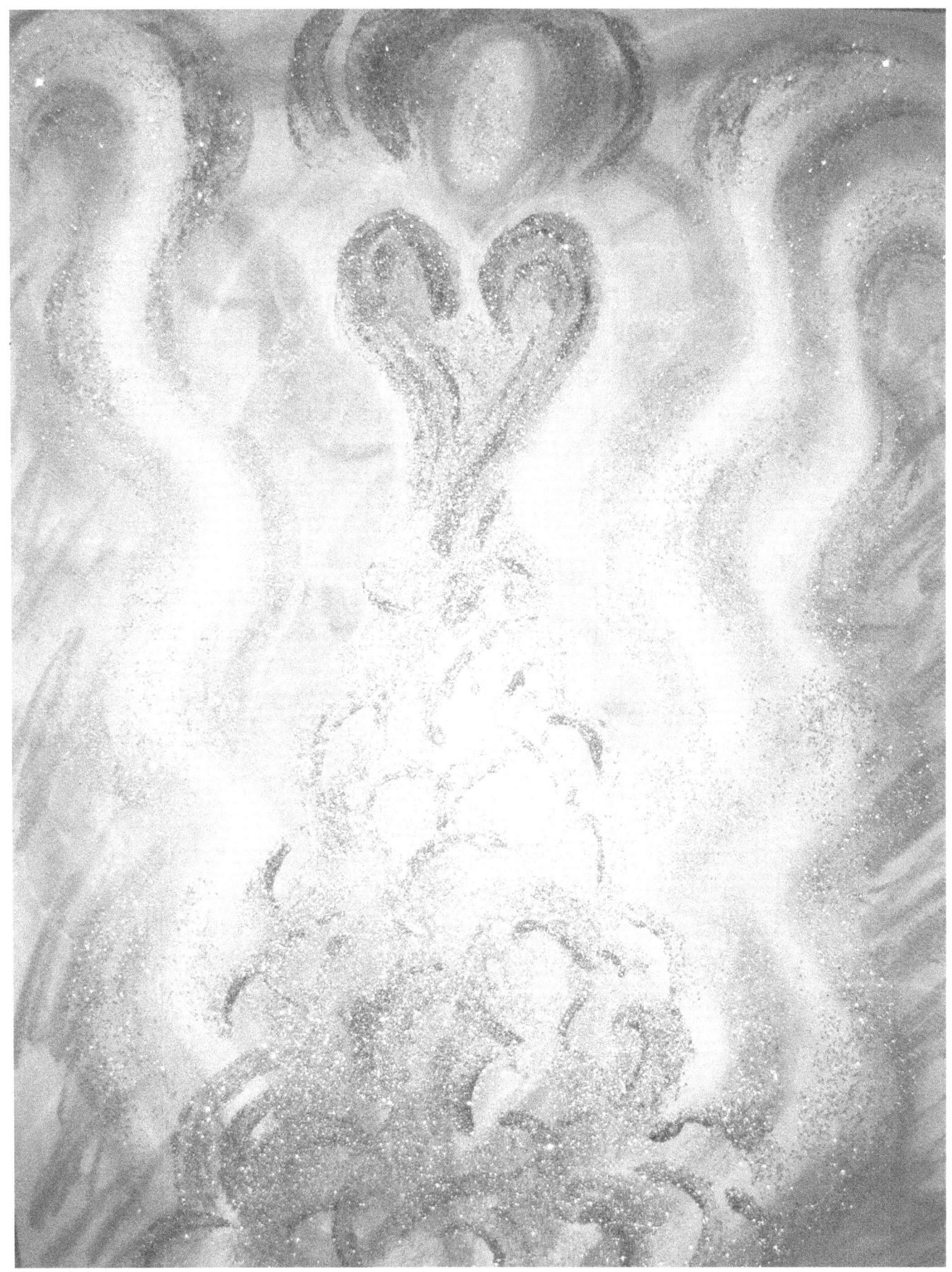

SPIRITUAL TRANSFORMATION ANGEL

If I Were A Color

If I were a color I would be Violet,
The Violet Flame of Spiritual Transformation

I would invoke the qualities of the Violet Flame, in each & every one of you,
Bringing forth a renewed sense of freedom and justice,
Forgiveness and mercy, and most of all joy.

I would use the Violet Flame as a tool
A tool to help raise the vibrational frequency of our planet,
To raise the conscious awareness of all its inhabitants,
To accelerate the spiritual growth of one and all.

I would call forth the Violet Flame
and in so doing let it impart a feeling of élan in each and every one of you —
A feeling of vibrancy, buoyancy and vitality.

And the impact of this Violet Flame would be so profound
it would liberate you, from all your fears,
It would empower you, with a renewed sense of self,
A desire to let your own light shine so brightly,
that others would not only be drawn to it, but be encouraged to do the same.

Yes, if I were a color I would be Violet …
The Violet Flame of Spiritual Transformation

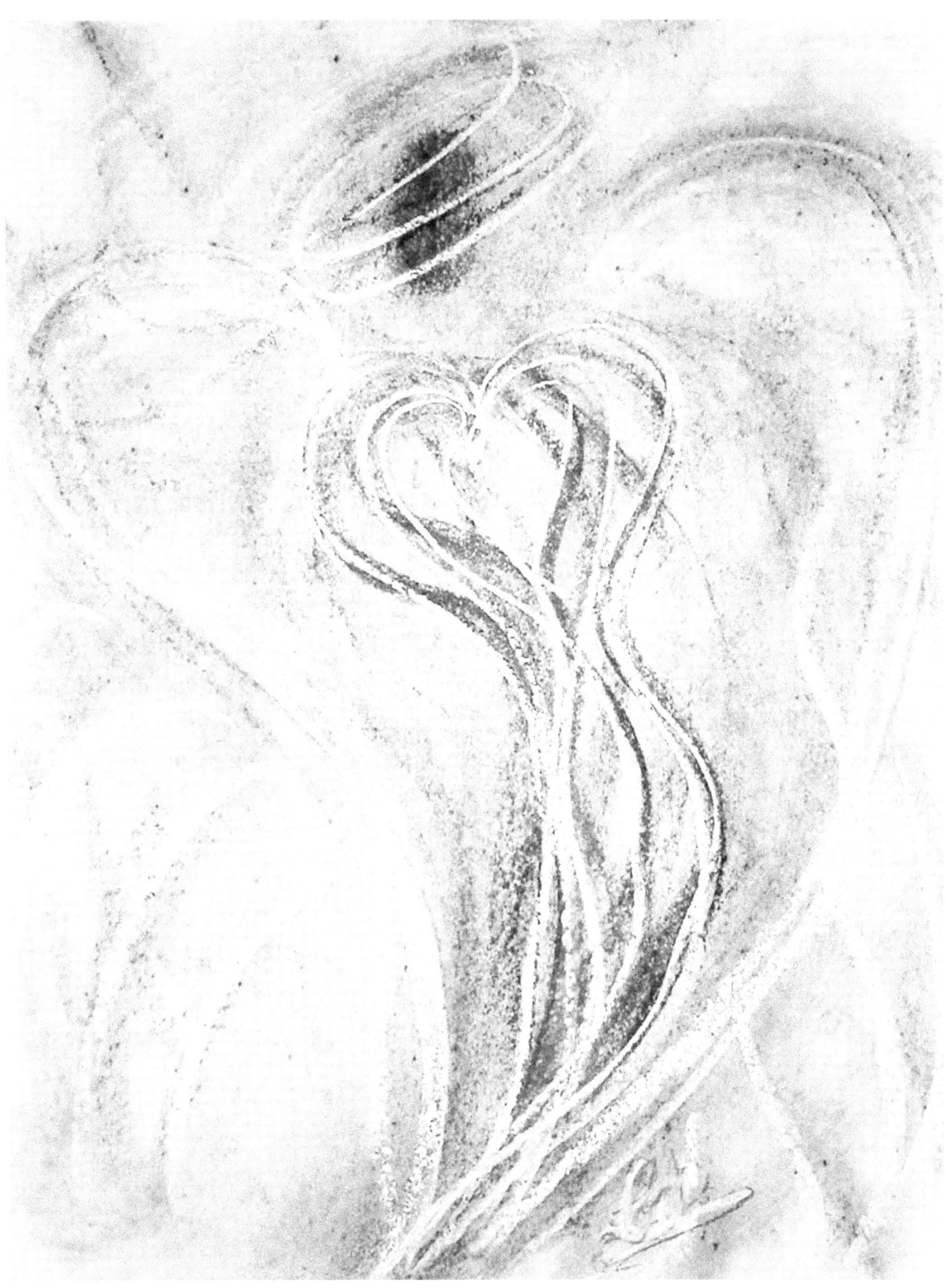

THE MULTI-DIMENSIONAL ANGEL

The Multi-Dimensional Angel's Message:

Most women, and some men, would consider themselves very adept at multitasking. This angel represents the multi-dimensional aspects of ourselves that enable us to do that. You know, like the conscious mind and the subconscious mind (that part of you that drives the car while you're thinking about everything else in the world or talking on the phone).

She reminds us of how amazingly bright the light of our soul is. Her goal is to show us that we go on and on ... to infinity ... and to help us tap into those "other worldly" aspects of ourselves while here in a physical body. She reminds us that we are spiritual beings, having a human experience.

Focus on that higher aspect of yourself as you use ethereal colors to tap into the spiritual aspect of your being. Manifesting your heart's desires is so much easier from this elevated state.

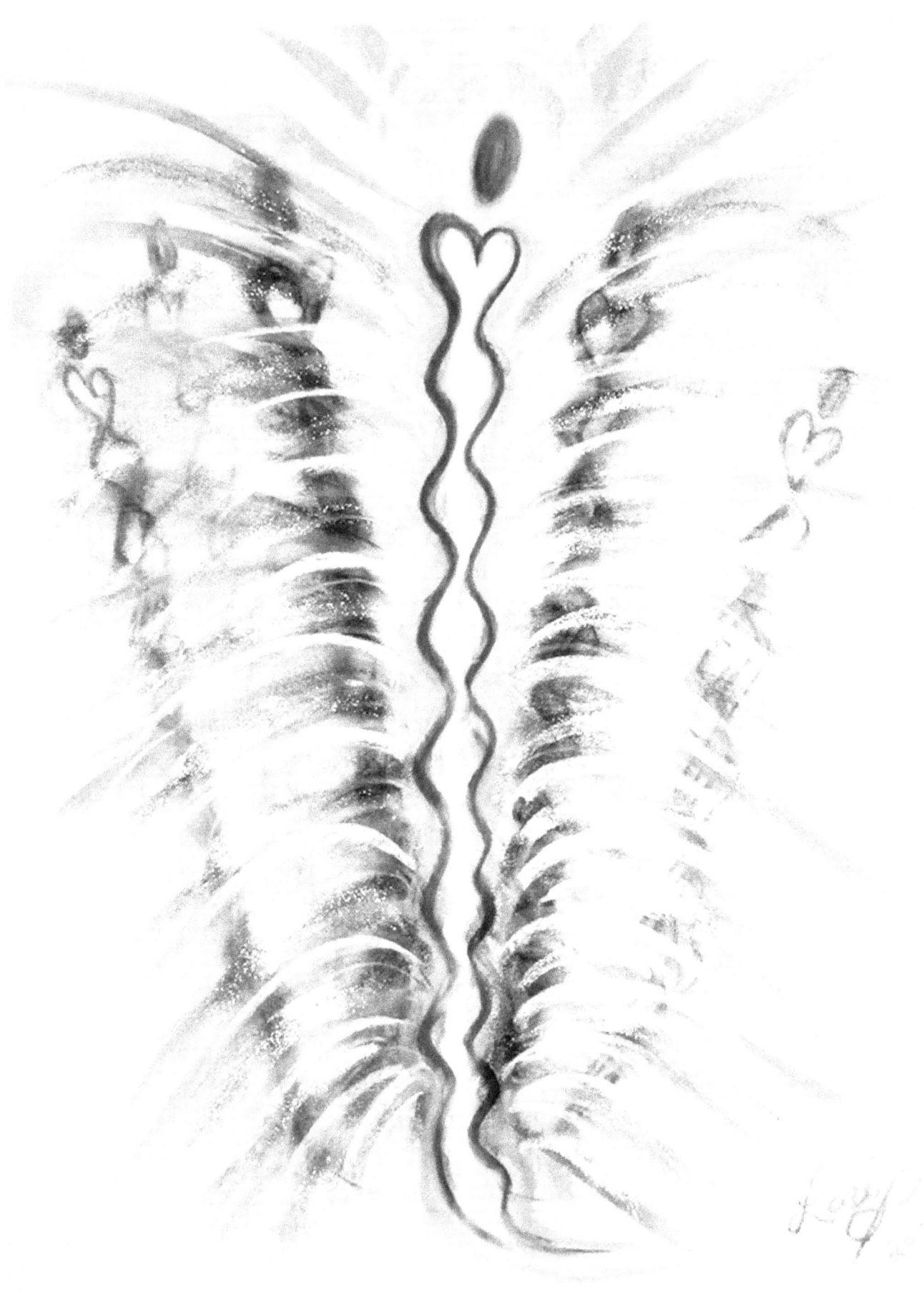

THE ANGEL OF PASSION

The Angel of Passion's Message ...

The angels say, "If you only knew what we go through to coordinate the intricacies of your lives you would be so amazed, especially your romantic relationships. We understand the enormity these relationships play in your personal growth and development. Our goal is to ensure the appropriateness of these experiences ... with of course, the appropriate people ... many of whom you've known in a prior life."

A compassionate heart is essential for the existence of true love. This Angel of Passion was designed to help you understand that compassion is not only reserved for those around you, it begins with feeling true compassion and deep seated love for yourself. To attract the relationship that's right for you, you must understand that compassion and love for yourself is the first and foremost step to finding true love.

Focus on Self Love as you passionately bring life and color to this angel.

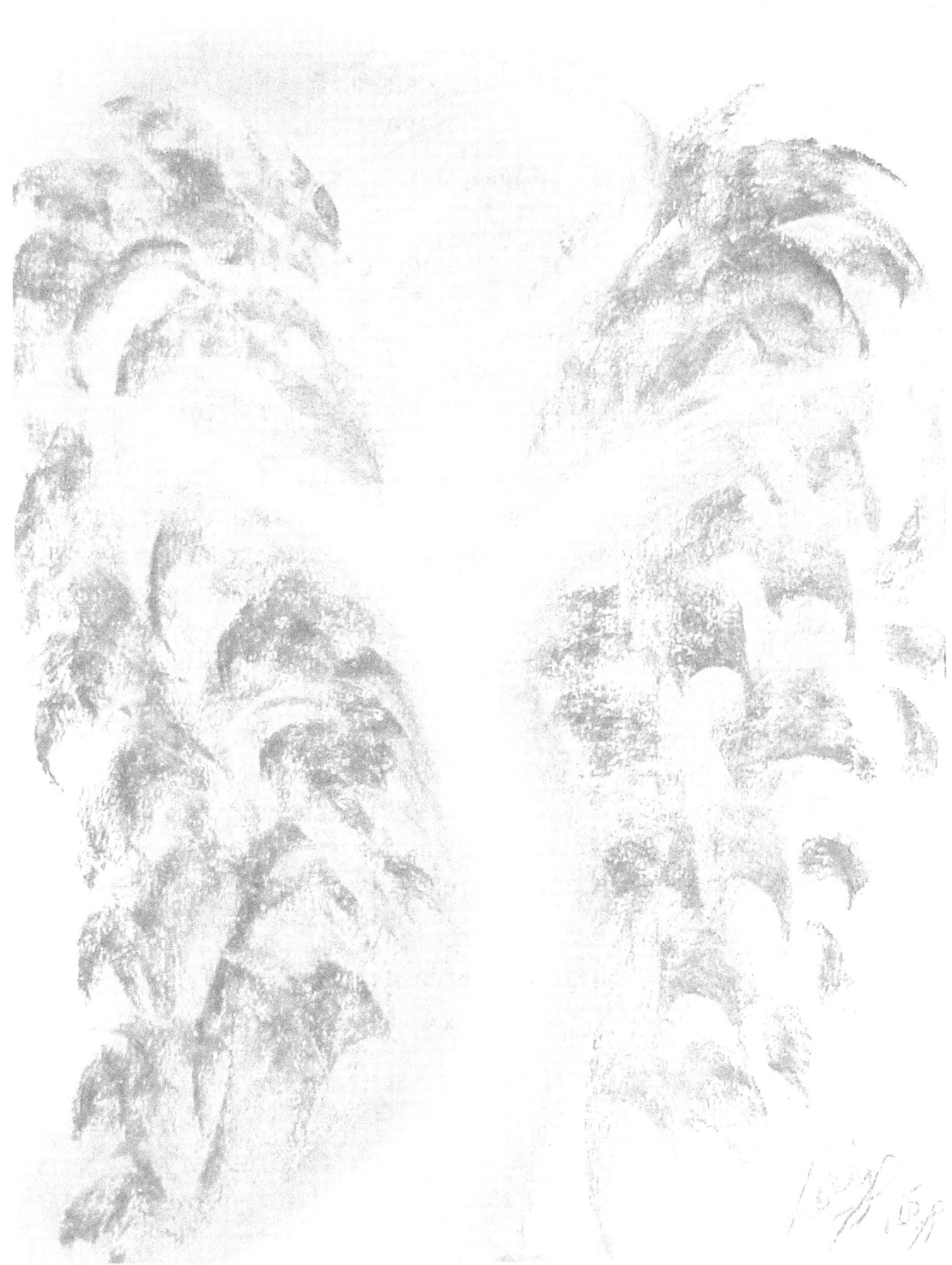

THE GOLDEN ONE

The Golden One on Vibrational Frequency ...

Recent breakthroughs have allowed researchers to measure a person's energetic frequency on a specific Vibrations Scale. Imagine a scale that ranges from 1 – 1,000. Muscle testing and kinesiology are used to determine where people are on this scale. All energy levels below 200 tested weak or life draining. Calibrations above 200 on the other hand are life affirming.

The average person vibrates somewhere in the vicinity of 175, a level where pride rules their life. The level we should aim for, however, is 500 and above. 500 is the vibration of love. At this level, healing occurs and one sees others as themselves. When you vibrate at this level life becomes drastically different. Love, joy, and abundance are suddenly within your grasp. Pain, stress, and struggle seem to melt away. At this level you literally become a magnet for what you truly desire.

This angel, referred to simply as the Golden One, was created to help those who are ready move through their emotional blocks and limiting beliefs ... those things that are no longer serving them. It's goal is to raise your frequency to 540, the level of gold, where love becomes unconditional.

Color your way to becoming a golden light of love and joy
                              ~ ~ A beautiful, magnificent place to be.

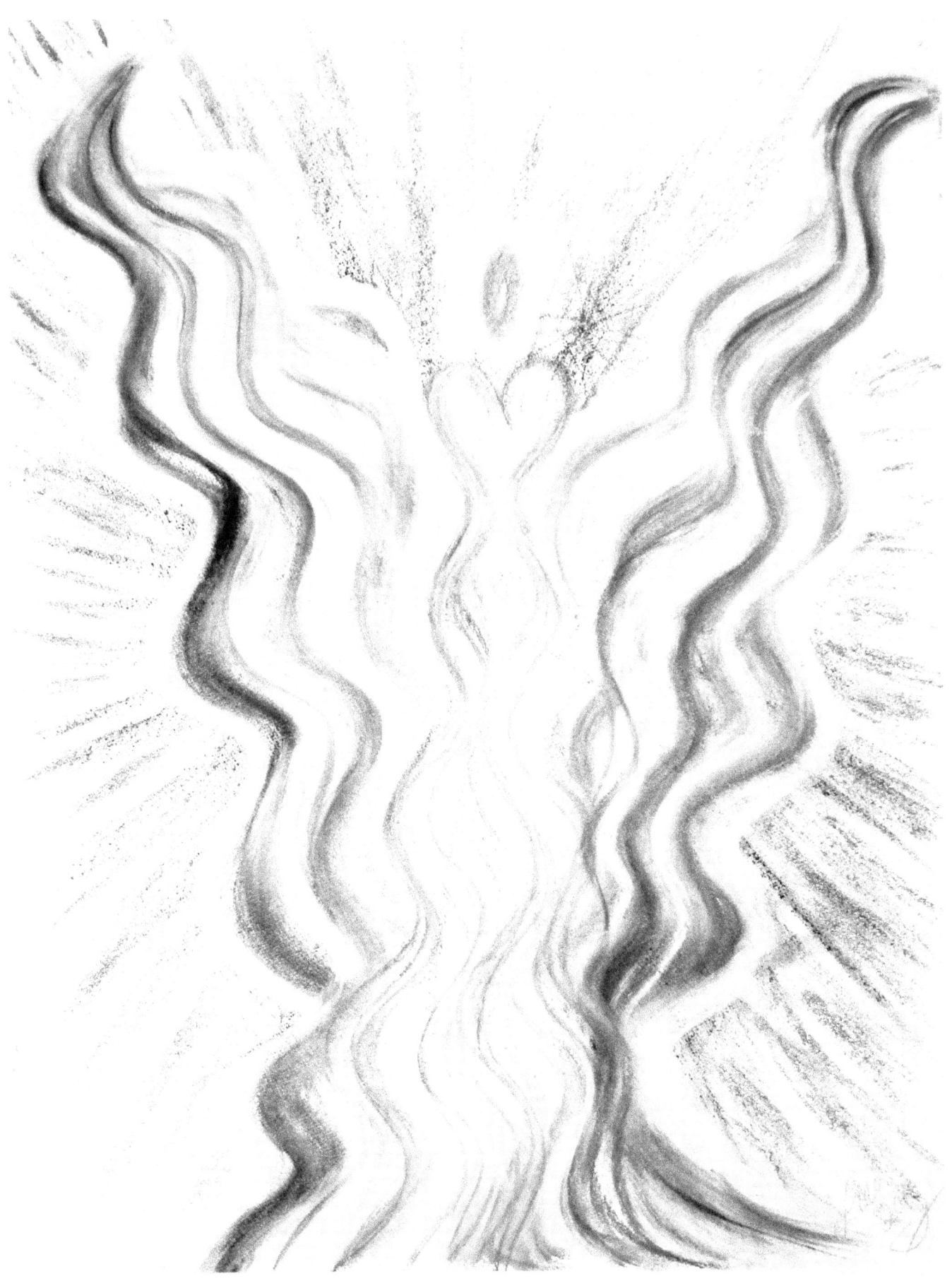

THE SOUL INTEGRATION ANGEL

Are You Doing What You Came Here to Do?

Indigenous spiritual and cultural traditions teach us that each of us came here with a purpose. In other words we came with a "gift" to bring to the world. Some cultures even select a name for the child that reflects this gift; reminding the child each time its name is spoken, what they came here to do.

We in modern societies are not raised with the wisdom of these ancient traditions. Rather than being encouraged to be "all that we (personally) can be", most of us are simply filled with the "shoulds" of life ... We should go to college ... get married ... get a great job with fabulous benefits. These "shoulds" often feel like we've sold our soul to the devil. It's really not the devil we're being sold to, it's just that we're selling ourselves short.

Few of us were ever asked what was in our hearts to do ... or what our souls were yearning for. And very few of us were ever encouraged to follow that wise all knowing guidance that lies deep in our hearts.

So dream as you color the Soul Integration Angel and she will help you unlock the wisdom and inner knowing of what you came here to do ...
and begin to live a life you truly love.

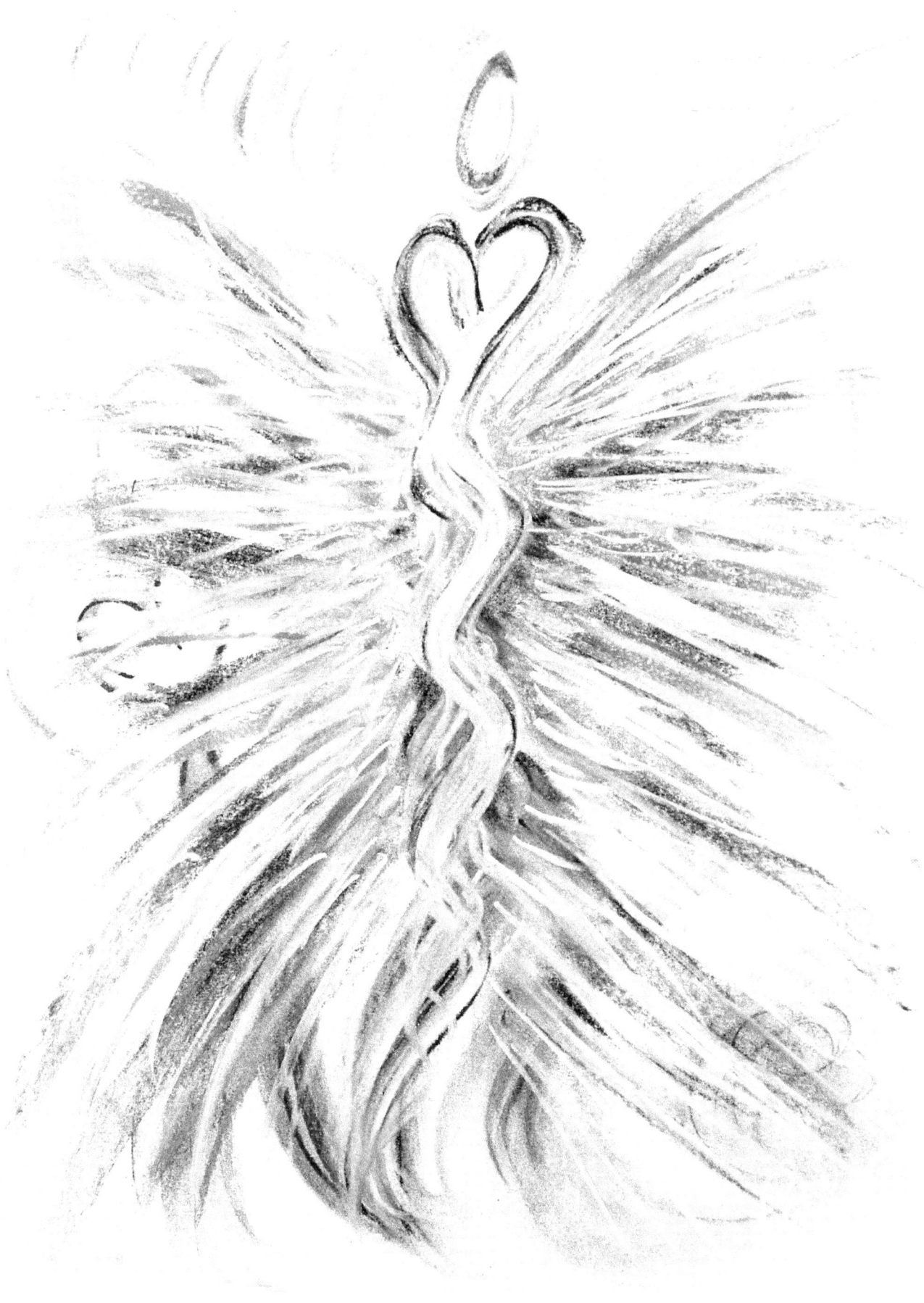

Divine Feminine Wisdom Angel

The Wisdom of the Divine Feminine ...

Your softness is your strength ... Yes, my dear, it is that simple.

The Goddess represents the divine embodied in nature, in human beings, in the flesh. The Goddess is not one image but many -- Maiden, Mother, and Crone. Our femininity is what attracts a mate and helps us to procreate. Yet in the end it is our wisdom we are worshipped for.

Color this angel with softness and let her bring forth the Creative Goddess that lies within YOU.

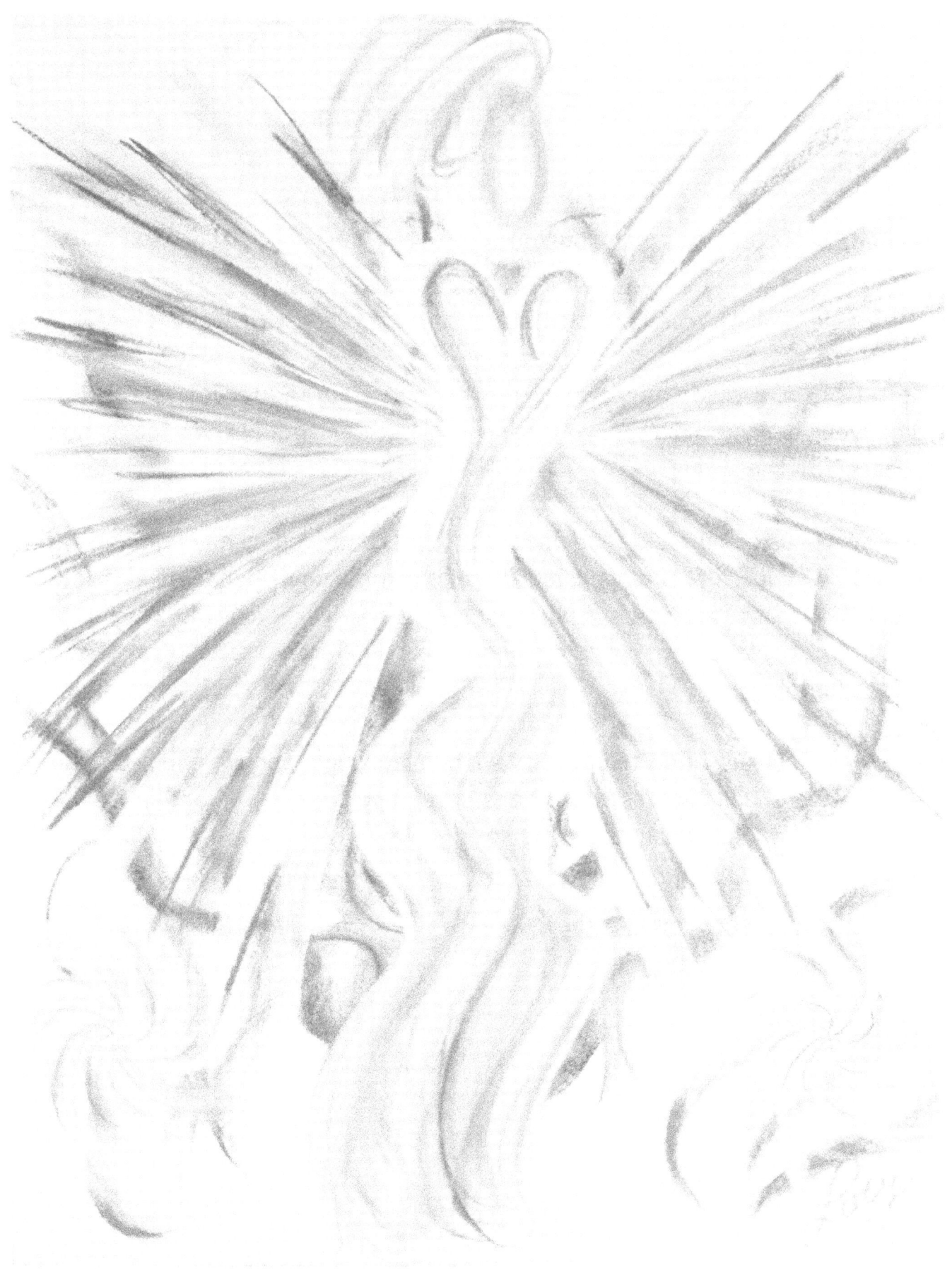

The Soul Mate Angel

Soul Mate Angel's Message for You...

"The expression of true love is what your heart yearns for," she says.

She tells us the first thing to realize when choosing to attract your twin flame, your perfect partner, your lover and best friend, is that you are both an aspect of the divine.

She advises us to put aside judgments of others as well as any unworthy thoughts of yourself, and open your heart to the magnificence of all that is. When you accept that you are both parts of the divine, you will come to understand the need for extreme kindness and gentleness, both for yourself and those you love.

Once your heart is filled to capacity with love, simply open it and send that amazing love energy across the ethers, intending that it will land in the heart of your beloved, and know that it is so.

Color this angel with the colors of love.

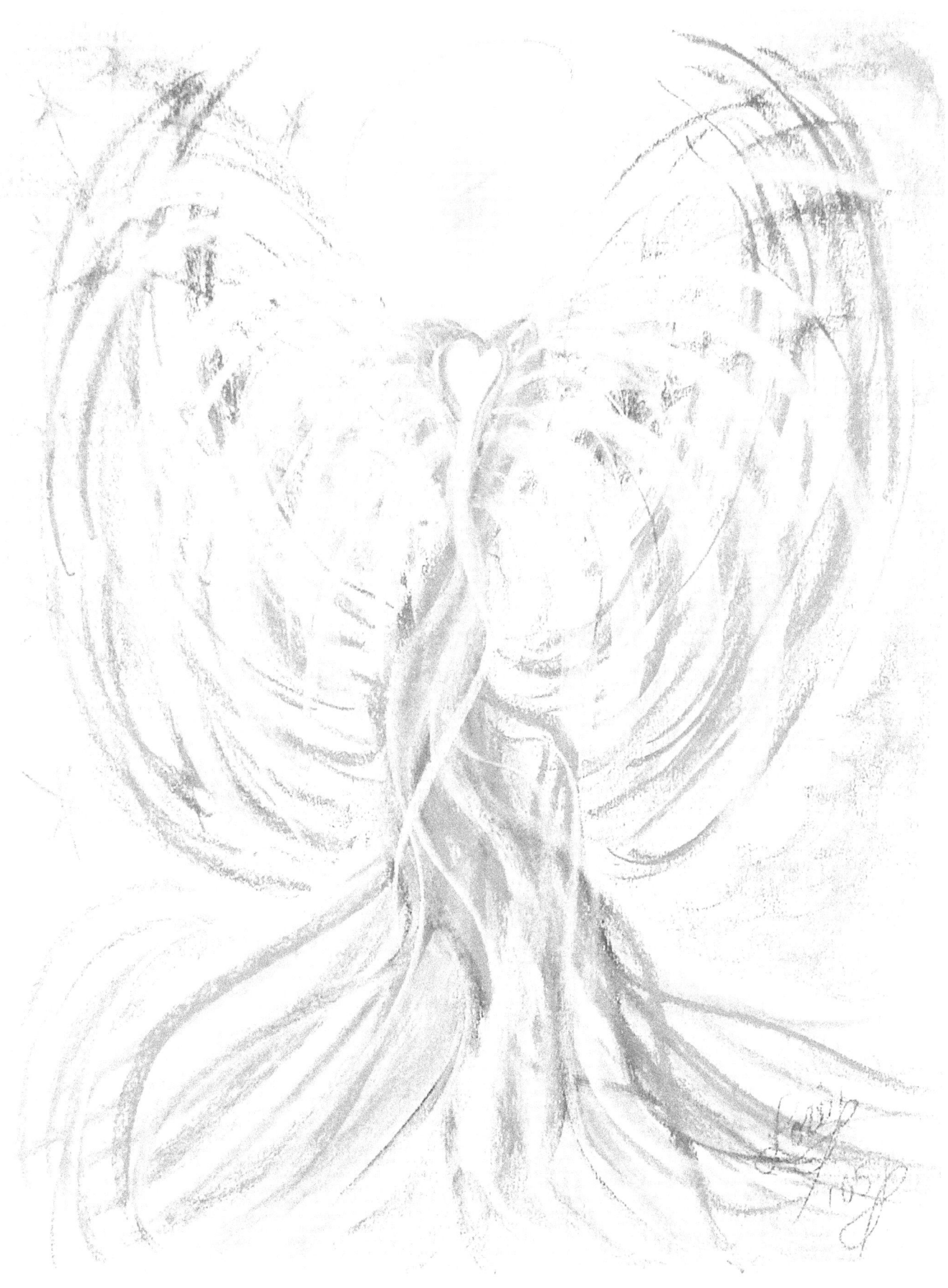

Higher Consciousness Angels

The Higher Consciousness Angels are perfect for anyone looking to better themselves and the world around them.

They want you to know that on average 90 -98% of the time we are "reacting" from our subconscious mind, rather than consciously choosing or "acting" with our higher consciousness mind.

Why is this important?

Because we are creating our destinies every moment of every day by the thoughts we think and the emotions we feel, making it imperative that we stay more consciously aware of those very thoughts and feelings to create the life we are truly dreaming of.

We must focus on what it is we are wanting, and let go of worry, to attract more magic into our lives.

Imagine what your perfect life looks like and color these angels in those magical colors you envision.

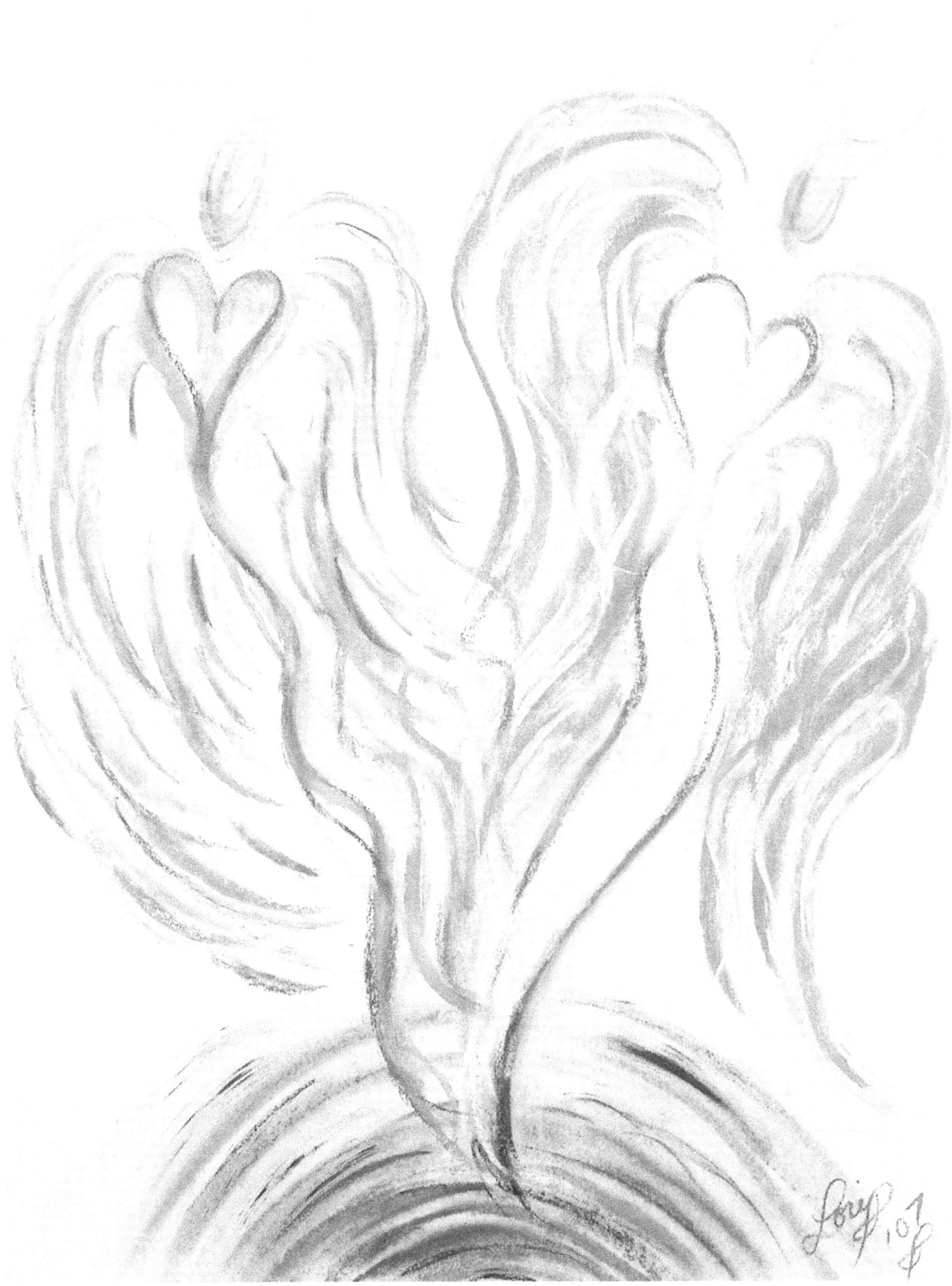

Angel of Hope

The Angel of Hope reminds us that we have the power to resolve things that seem to be bothering us. As spiritual beings, having a human experience, we need only remember who we really are and put our power into action.

The first thing we must do is stop buying into the illusion of the situation. Rather than listening to the critics, naysayers and skeptics, and believing that the sky is falling, perhaps we should remember what is truth. And the truth of the matter is that things aren't really falling apart; rather they are changing, growing and evolving into something so much grander and greater than anything we have ever known.

It's simply time to do things better. It's not a revolution we're seeking, it's a kinder, gentler, more loving approach to life that we're after. We must get a crystal clear picture of what we'd like our world, and our lives, to look like. We must believe with all our heart and all our soul that we can have what it is we are wanting. In fact, we have to believe it so much that we can actually feel the excitement of how we will feel when we actually have it.

Let this Angelic Message Portrait be your talisman for Hope.
Let her bring you comfort in time of need, peace in times of turmoil, and most important of all, let her replace fear with the healing power of love.

Comfort colors are what this angel needs most. Give her yours …

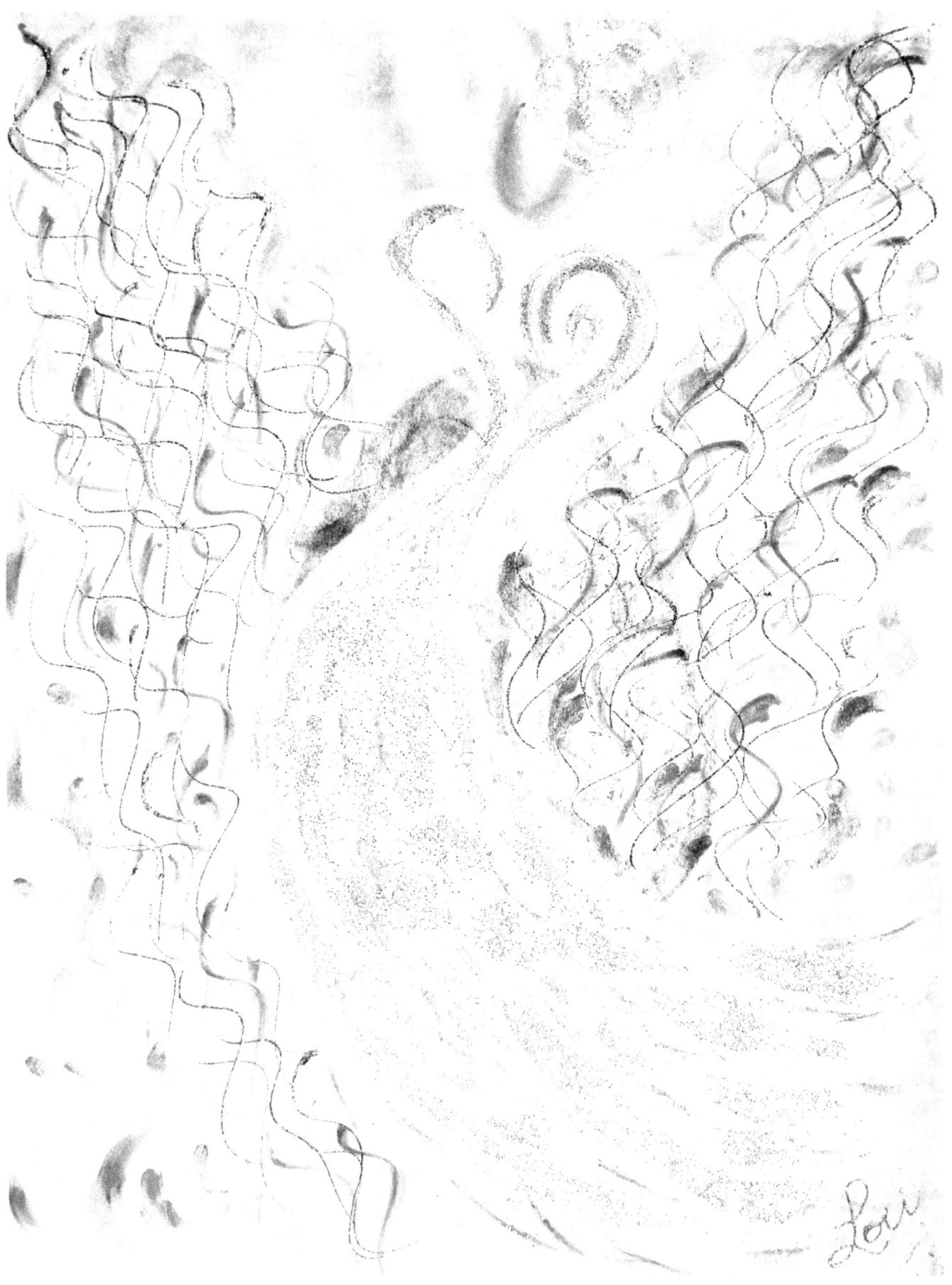

The Positive Attitude Angel

The Angels tell us the surest way to achieving and maintaining a healthy positive attitude is to let go of that which is no longer serving us. We need to go deep within ourselves and do an emotional house cleaning.

Once that is accomplished we are free and clear to follow our hearts. For it is in the following of our heart's desires that we will find true joy.

When we open ourselves to that divinely inspired passion we will know we have found not just the right path, but our path.

It is then, the angels remind us, that we are to not get caught up in the details of how this will be accomplished. For ours is not to determine how . . . ours is simply to allow.

Let this Positive Attitude Angel help you find and follow the passion that burns within your heart.

Fuel her energy with the colors you are most passionate about!

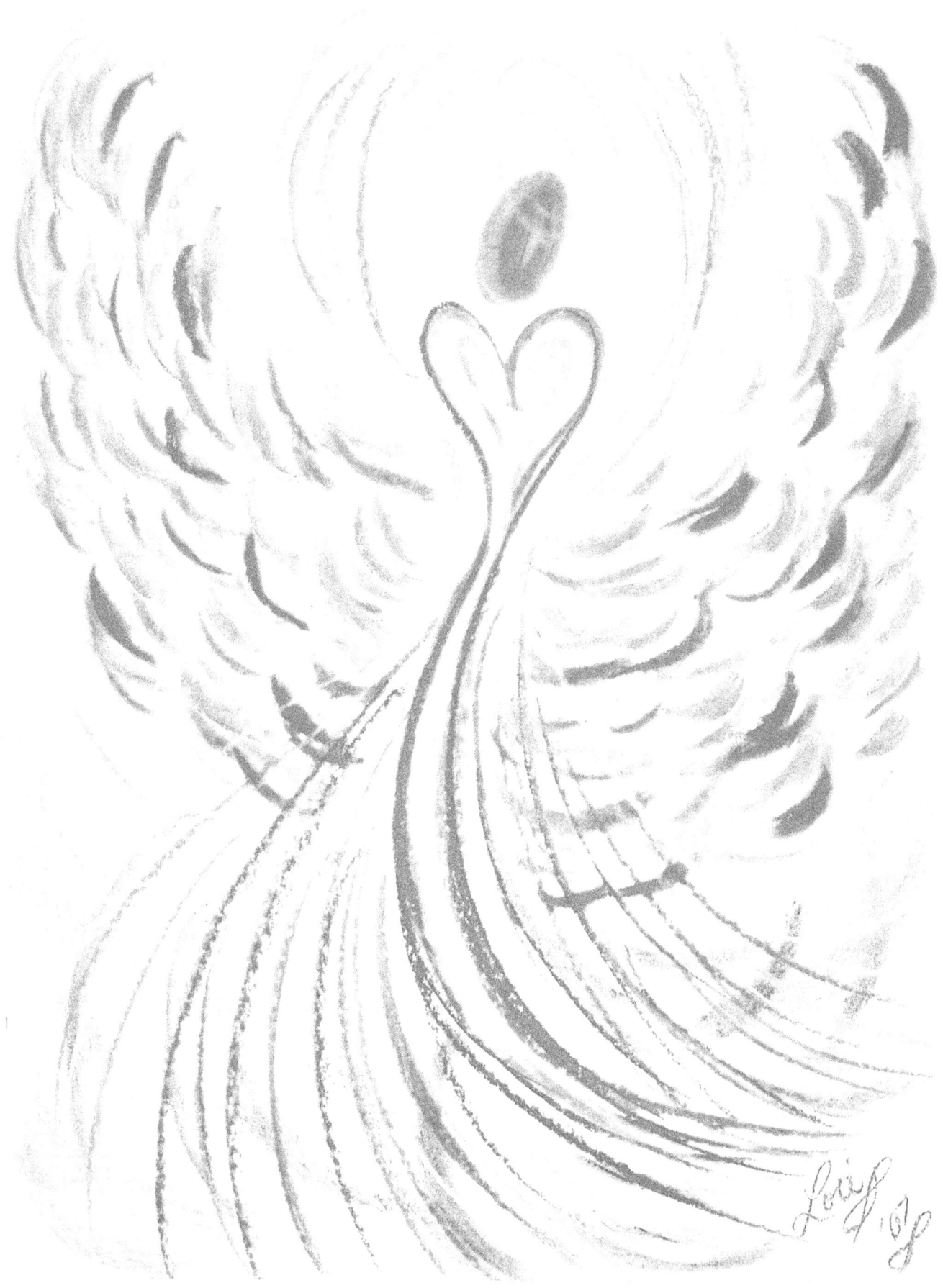

All is Well Angel

The All is Well Angel's Message for You...

When I asked the angels the most simple and direct question of all, "What does the world need to know NOW?" I received the most simple and direct answer, "All is well ... all is in divine order."

What we often perceive as chaos and unrest, is often simply the answer to our prayers. Times of change can seem upsetting and unruly, for as we are asking for and anxiously anticipating the change we want to occur, we are being separated from that which is old and comfortable. It may not be what we want anymore, but it's like an old shoe that's broken in and easy to walk in ... and often very hard to throw away.

So the angels tell us to breathe deeply ... get plenty of exercise ... spend time in nature ... meditate ... and gently allow ourselves the time to adjust to this higher, and oh so desired, newness we so desire.

Comfort colors are what this angel calls for ...
                                    those very colors that comfort your soul.

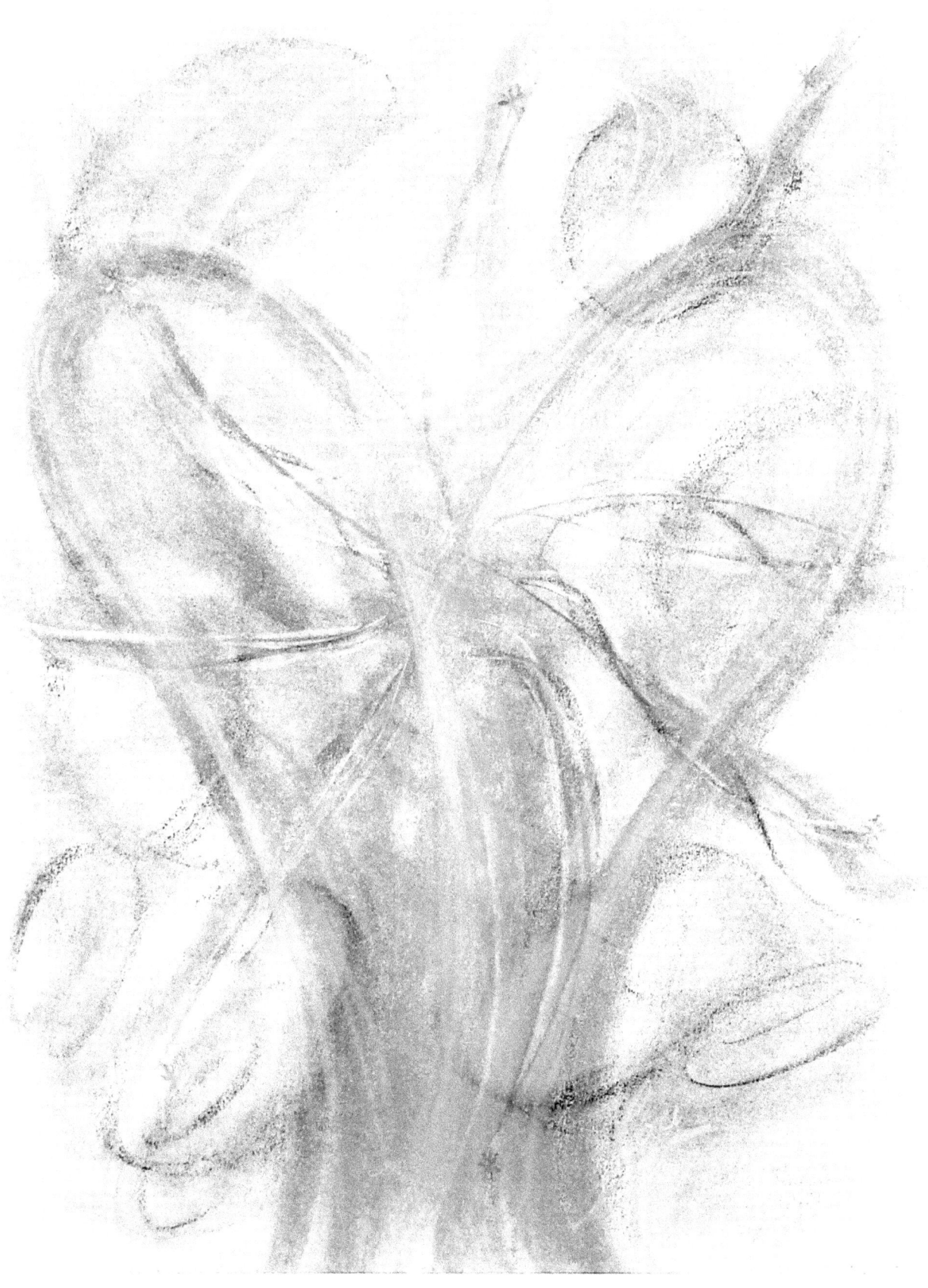

The Angel of Allowing

Angel of Allowing's Message for you...

Grace and ease is this angel's mantra. Like the Law of Allowing, this angel reminds us to stay in the flow ... to take the path of least resistance ... to "allow" the universe to support us as we move along on our journeys.

"Notice what's showing up that's new," she says. "Observe what's working ... as something always is. Notice if it feels like you are swimming upstream, or gently floating down stream with the current of the river of life. The natural rhythm of life works effortlessly with nature. We are always supported by the divine loving angels that surround us ... all we need do is get out of our ego selves and allow love to flow all around us.

Let this Angel of Allowing help you relax into the ebbs and flows of life with grace and ease.

Let the beauty of nature inspire you as you effortlessly color her beautiful.

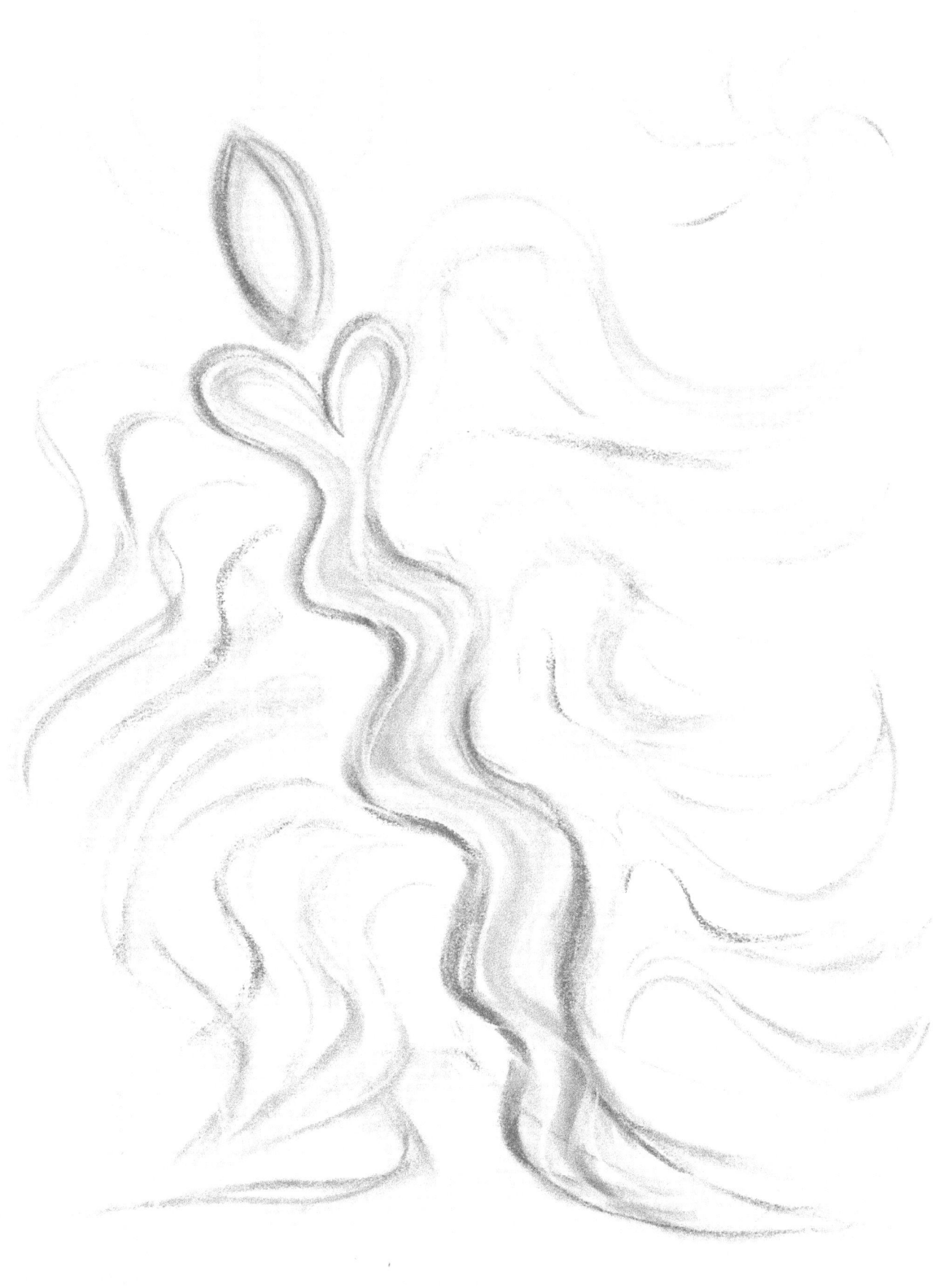

The Winter Solstice Angels

Winter Solstice Angels' Messages for You …

A few years back on the eve of the Winter Solstice, I posed this question,

"What do we need to do to assist with "bringing in the light" and helping to awaken the collective consciousness of mankind?"

The answer was a wake up call for earth angels everywhere. Shoot for the moon and if you miss at least you'll land amongst the stars. So dream big and follow the guidance that will unfold for you one step at a time. Then set your intention to accomplish that goal … and TRUST that the universe will support you in all ways.

Focus on the Ascension Attitudes of Love, Surrender and Gratitude … Let go of the fears and limiting beliefs that no longer serve you or your life.

As you do your spirits will lift, you will feel lighter and brighter. You will become a way shower, an excellent example of how to be a spiritual being having a human experience.

Pretend now that it is a winter's eve on the darkest day of the year and let your coloring bring in the light.

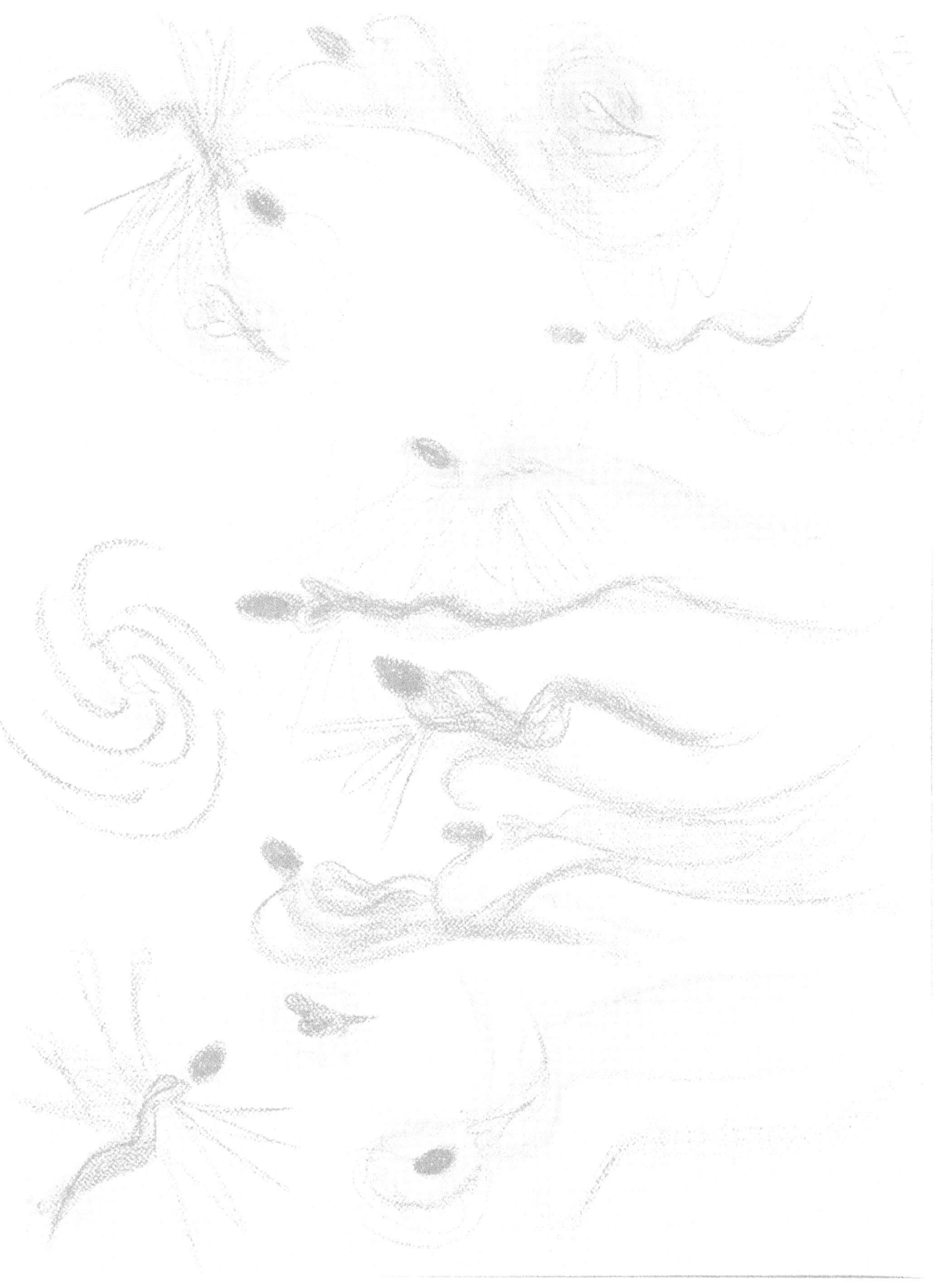

ABOUT THE AUTHOR

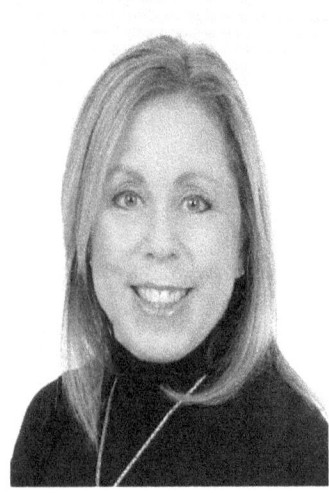

New Thought Leader, Lori Daniel Falk is an Epigenetic Healing Artist, Author, and Coach who has been gifted with an artistic healing modality that enables her to communicate with, and share, the wisdom of the angels in both pictures and words. Her Angelic Message Portraits™ are not just images of beauty, they are epigenetic tools designed to heal at a deep emotional level. They bring a feeling of wonderment and inspiration to all who view them. To date they have found homes in 25 countries around the world, have graced the covers of numerous magazines, have been a regular feature on the DailyOm and are exhibited at Hay House Publishing conferences across the country.

Ms. Falk, a graduate of the School of Spiritual Psychology, is a Certified Spiritual Life Coaching and Reiki Master. She has been a featured guest on both radio and TV. Her book, *"What the World Needs to Know NOW, Wisdom of the Angels,"* is available at www.wisdomoftheangels.com. Her new line of Greeting Cards are currently being test-marketed by Blue Mountain Arts.

Prior to embarking on this spiritual journey, Ms. Falk was the editor and publisher of the international trade publication RTW Review (Ready-to-Wear Review) providing retailers with the fashion industry's pertinent monthly news. Utilizing her years of experience as a fashion buyer and retail manager, as well as her expertise in sighting emerging trends, she was often referred to as the "go to" person in the retail fashion industry. During that time she wrote a series of books on retailing including *"Electronic Commerce: How to Sell on the Net," "Resort Retail, Attracting Today's Busy Woman," "Capitalizing on the Billion $$$ Airport Retail Market,"* and *"Retailing in Today's World."*

"Michael Jackson once said, 'I believe that all art has as it's ultimate goal, the union between the material and the spiritual, the human and the divine.' This fully describes my art. Through the use of pastel chalks, mineral pigments and illuminating glitter paints I am able to capture the healing energy of the divine in angelic portraits that engage the viewer through their use of vibrant color and reflective light, while simultaneously enabling them to assimilate the "Wisdom of the Angels" directly into their emotional field by igniting their hearts."

-- Lori Daniel Falk

Angelic Message Portraits™

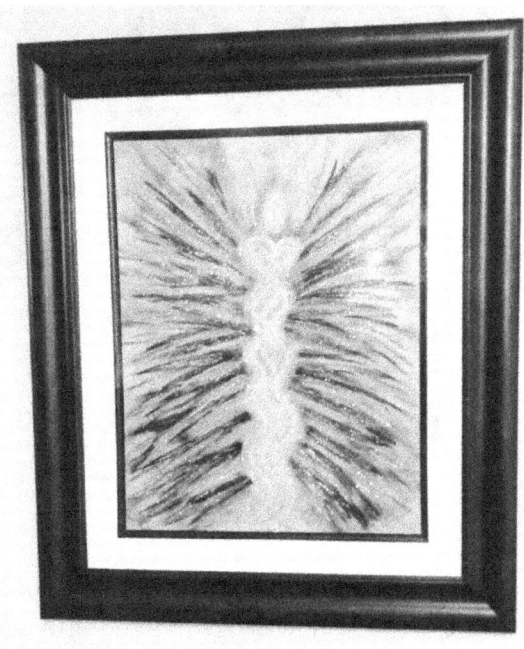

Lori Daniel Falk, an Epigenetic Healing Artist, has been gifted with a new artistic healing modality designed to clear your emotional ancestral DNA, helping you to alleviate "dis-ease." Lori creates Angelic Message Portraits™ that are encoded with powerful emotional healing energy designed to work with you at a heart level to heal your emotions. This channeled artwork contains the benevolent loving energy of the angels.

Your custom Angelic Message Portrait will start with a complete angel reading on the subject of your choice, or we'll ask the angels want you need to know at this time to experience more love, joy, health, wealth, peace and happiness. The energy of that wisdom then gets encoded into a portrait designed to work with you at a heart level. The finished piece is actually an Angelic representation of the YOU, you are becoming.

TO SCHEDULE YOUR APPOINTMENT

Experience the healing power of this angelic art for yourself.
Pre-pay for your appointment NOW and get a FREE Matted Art Print!

http://wisdomoftheangels.com/custom-angelic-message-portraits/

Angelic Rx's Adult Coloring Book Series

by Epigenetic Healing Artist, Lori Daniel Falk

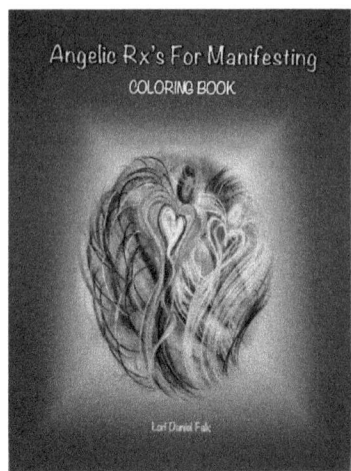

Relax & Color

Help, I need to relax ... Then COLOR, it's that easy! Seems the latest craze in relaxation techniques has nothing to do with meditating or yoga, and everything to do with color and visual pleasure.

Our new *Angelic Rx's Adult Coloring Book*s allow you to experience the wisdom of the angels while you focus on living the life of your dreams. Inside each you'll find 20 angelic art activities that will take you to a calm, peaceful and happy place of coloring bliss. These angelic images offer an easy way to de-stress and unleash your inner artist. Plus, each one has a message from the angels to assist you in your dream creation.

Coming Soon ...

Angelic Rx's for JOY (August 2016) Reg. Price $14.99

  Order Now & SAVE ... Pre-Publication only $7.99, plus $4.99 shipping

Angelic Rx's for an Amazing Life (October 2016) Reg. Price $14.99

  Order Now & SAVE ... Pre-Publication only $7.99, plus $4.99 shipping

3 **B**ook **S**et at Pre-Publication Special $24.99, plus $9.99 shipping/handling.

www.wisdomoftheangels.com

Products for Angel Lovers Everywhere

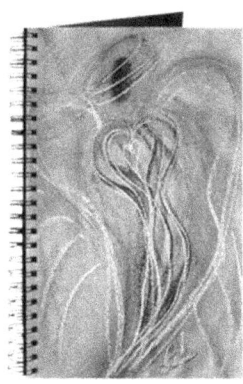 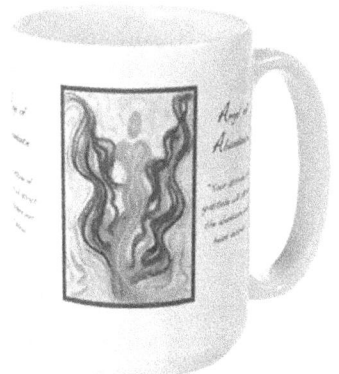 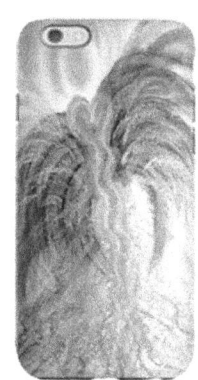

We now offer the Angelic Message Portraits™ featured in Lori's book, *"What the World Needs to Know NOW, Wisdom of the Angels"* in a variety of options from Ornaments and Angel Journals to Coffee Mugs and Accent Pillows.

Each of these "angels" were created not just as an image of beauty, but as an energetic healing tool ... designed to assist with social issues and wellness concerns, as well as your own personal growth and development. We have found that the reproduced art carries the strength of the original portraits; making these items so much more than what they seem ... they are in fact, transformational healing tools.

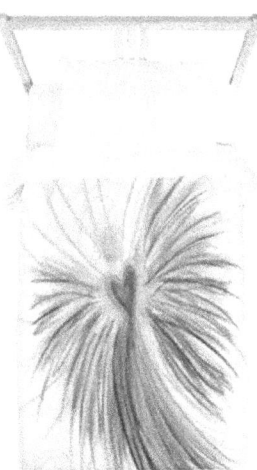

Enjoy them yourself ... gift them to a friend ... and know, each time you do,you are spreading the love of the angels one person at a time ...

http://wisdomoftheangels.com/online-store/

www.ingramcontent.com/pod-product-compliance
Lightning Source LLC
Chambersburg PA
CBHW080836170526
45158CB00009B/2575

* 9 7 8 0 6 9 2 6 8 3 1 2 5 *